SEA LIFE
FIELD GUIDE

DOVER

Dover Publications, Inc.
Mineola, New York

Bibliographical Note

Sea Life Field Guide, first published by Dover Publications, Inc., in 2013,
is a new compilation of both new and revised published material.

International Standard Book Number

ISBN-13: 978-0-486-49157-8
ISBN-10: 0-486-49157-9

Manufactured in the United States by LSC Communications
49157903   2020
www.doverpublications.com

Layout and Design by Hourglass Press

Sea Life

About 71 percent of the world's surface is covered in oceans or seas, and due to their depth, they contain about 300 times the habitable space as dry land. More than 230,000 different species of sea life have been documented, but marine biologists predict that they number in the millions.

The species range from microscopic plankton to whales, the largest animals on earth. There is also a great variety of fish, whales, reptiles, jellyfish, anemones, mollusks, coral, crabs, and other crustaceans and arthropods.

There is a wide variety of aquatic ecosystems spanning different temperatures and depths, and each of these ecosystems supports a different range of sea life. While nutrient-heavy coastal waters are home to the majority of known species, there is still much life in the deeper, largely unexplored ocean. Most notably, coastal waters are home to coral reefs, which support vast numbers of sea creatures. The open ocean—beyond the continental shelf—doesn't have as many documented species, but plankton that inhabit the water closer to the surface support a wide array of fish and many migratory animals making ocean-wide treks. Though the open ocean covers a vast area and reaches extreme depths (up to 36,000 feet), it is also the least studied area of the ocean. Exploration of this area is still turning up new species regularly, even at the deepest depths, in areas previously believed uninhabitable.

Continued exploration of the oceans and their undiscovered habitats promises the discovery of millions of new marine species.

t a crab at

ving fossil

3

Whales & Dolphins

The striped dolphin is similar in size and shape to many dolphins, reaching about 8 feet in length. It can be found in oceans throughout the world. Generally, however, it is confined to warmer waters, where it often appears in schools of hundreds. Like other dolphins, it feeds largely on squid.

The Ganges River dolphin, or susu, is one of four species of freshwater dolphins. It's found only in the Ganges River of India and its tributaries. A very strange creature, it is virtually blind, never sleeps for more than a few seconds at a time, and swims, with its head constantly bobbing, on its right side and only in circles. It has also been reported to have bad breath.

The long-finned pilot whale is found in the North Atlantic Ocean and parts of the temperate Southern Hemisphere. Contrary to its name, it is technically a dolphin, not a whale. It's very sociable and congregates in herds of hundreds. This animal's name comes from its propensity to follow a leader (or pilot).

The beluga, or white whale, is not actually related to dolphins. It lacks a dorsal fin and is one of a few species of similarly sized toothed whales. The beluga has been called the "sea-canary" for the variety of odd sounds it emits. It lives in the ice-packed waters of the Arctic.

Hourglass Dolphin

This is a less-studied dolphin found only in the little-traveled Antarctic and subantarctic waters. The hourglass dolphin is black with two large white patches on either side that conjoin to resemble an hourglass.

Hourglass dolphins travel in groups of 5 to 10, but will merge with Antarctic whale groups who feed on the same animals.

Killer Whale

Also known as an orca, the killer whale is technically a dolphin. It is the largest predator of warm-blooded animals in the world. Hunting in packs, it has been known to kill even full-grown blue whales. It more commonly preys on smaller whales, dolphins, and seals, in addition to fish. More than just a fierce carnivore, the killer whale displays intelligence and social behavior as complex as any other dolphin, while generally being non-aggressive toward humans, which has made it popular in aquatic theme parks.

6

The <u>minke whale</u> is a baleen whale, which means that it has a plate in its mouth—called a baleen plate—for filtering food from water. It feeds by gulping large quantities of water, krill, and fish, and then pushing the water back out of its mouth while ingesting the food.

It grows to be 33½ feet long.

The rotund, grotesque-looking <u>right whale</u> is very slow moving and becomes encrusted in barnacles. Once very common, its numbers have been drastically reduced through hunting. The few that remain inhabit various cooler parts of the globe. The <u>pygmy right whale</u> (also pictured) is even rarer and found only in Antarctic and subantarctic waters

The <u>sperm whale</u> is the largest toothed animal on earth, reaching up to 65 feet long. It feeds primarily on giant and colossal squid, for which it has to dive to incredible depths (as deep as 2 miles!). The enormous head contains spermaceti oil and a complex of tubes and other tissue, all of which, it is believed, aid in the creature's adjustment to enormous pressures at great depths.

The <u>narwhal</u> is a small-to medium-sized whale with a distinctive tusk that's a source of centuries-old legends about unicorns. The ivory "horn" is actually a twisted, overgrown tooth, and can reach up to 9 feet in length! Nobody is sure what it is for.

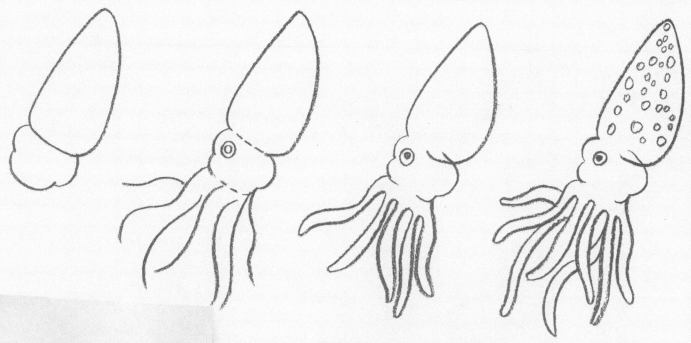

Most squid only get to be about **2** feet long, but giant and colossal squid can grow to over 46 feet long!

Squid

A squid is a cephalopod, a class of mollusk that also includes cuttlefish, octopuses, and nautiloidea. (Most of their related mollosks are snails!)

Squid have eight arms and two tentacles, all of which have suction cups and hooks. They have fins along the sides of their mantle (their body), but these fins aren't the primary source of propulsion. The squid's body contains a siphon that pulls in and expels water for jet propulsion. This enables the squid to move very quickly.

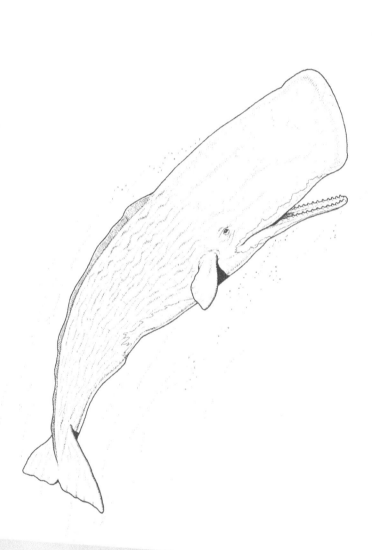

Squid are the food of
choice for sperm whales,
which eat about 3% of
their body weight per
day. That's a lot of squid!

Draw a school of squid
for this whale to dine on.

9

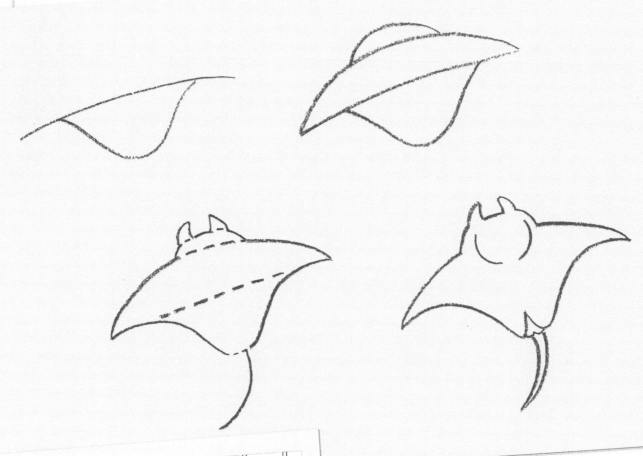

Manta Ray

Manta rays can be found in tropical and subtropical waters throughout the world. They reach enormous sizes, with "wingspans" of at least 25 feet.

Filter feeders, manta rays feed similarly to baleen whales, by gulping in water and filtering out the plankton. They will either swim through the open water, gulping it in, or eat plankton from the sea floor by scooping it up with the cephalic fins on either side of their mouths.

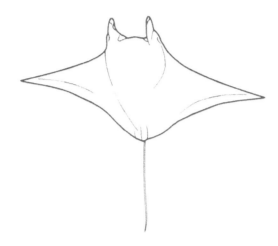

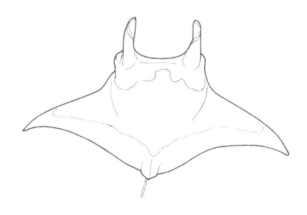

Manta rays travel in huge groups called "fevers." Some fevers are so large and dense that they seem to fill the entire visible ocean.

Complete this fever with as many manta rays as you can fit.

Moray Eel

Urchin

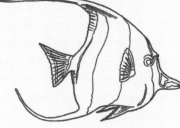

Moorish Idol

Clownfish

Seahorse

Scallop

Anemone

Starfish

Butterflyfish

Coral Crowds

Coral reefs are teeming with life. How many of the animals above can you find?

Reef Fish

Coral reefs are incredibly large and diverse ecosystems. They cover less than 0.1% of the ocean floor, but contain 25% of all marine species. These include some of the most colorful and beautiful tropical fish in the ocean.

Extremely colorful and unique, and commonly found in tropical reefs, the Moorish idol is a prime example of a tropical reef fish. These fish have skinny disk-like bodies, snouts, and relatively small fins, except for the dorsal fin, which is a trailing crest called a philomantis extension. Interestingly, the fin gets shorter with age.

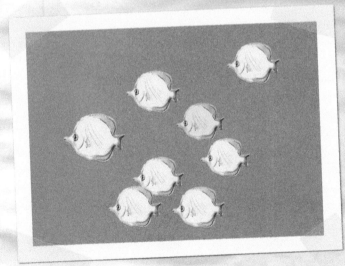

Fish of the family Chaetodontidae are commonly known as <u>butterfly fish,</u> and include a lot of what people think of as "tropical fish." Their name comes from their color and patterns, which can resemble a butterfly.

This family of fish includes around 120 species, which vary greatly in coloration and patterns, including a couple that look very similar to the Moorish idol (which does not fall into this family). They're mostly around $4\frac{1}{2}$ to $8\frac{1}{2}$ inches in length.

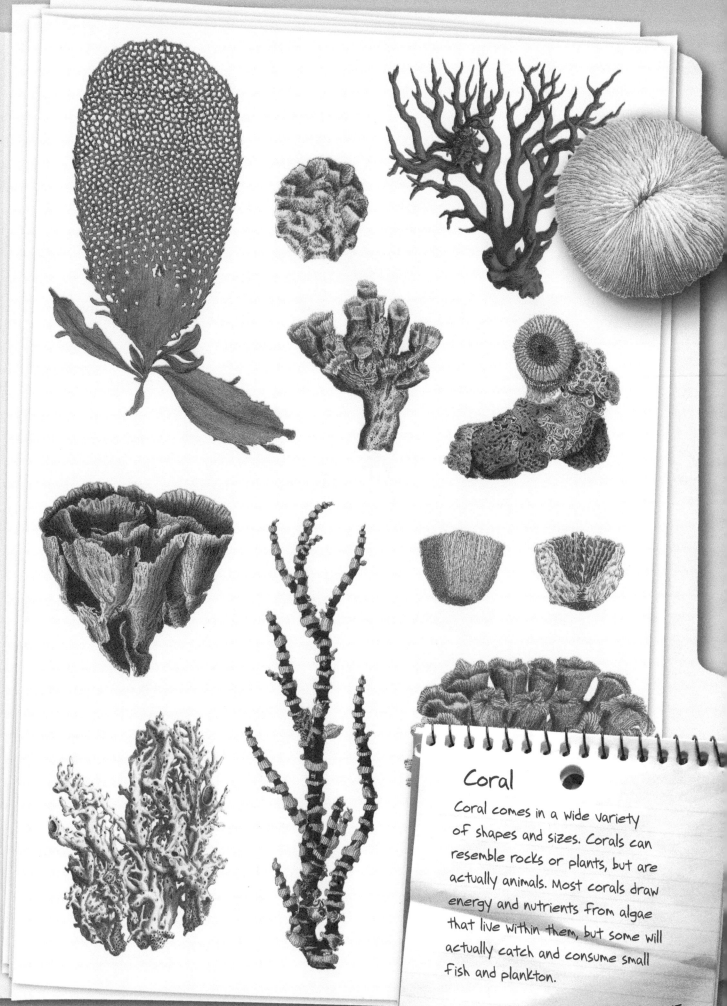

Coral

Coral comes in a wide variety of shapes and sizes. Corals can resemble rocks or plants, but are actually animals. Most corals draw energy and nutrients from algae that live within them, but some will actually catch and consume small fish and plankton.

15

A group of barracuda is called a "battery."

The green moray eel (top) and goldentail moray eel (bottom) are both found in the Caribbean Sea.

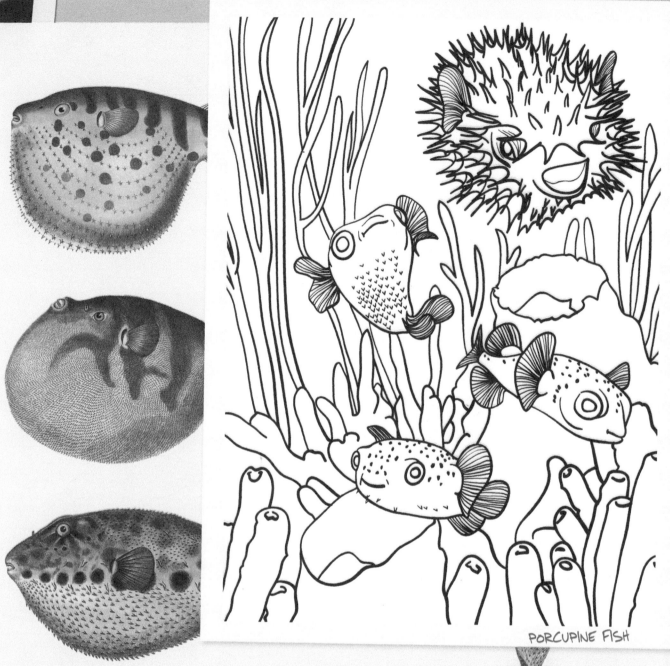

PORCUPINE FISH

"Blowfish"

There are numerous species of fish that have the ability to inflate their bodies. These fish are commonly referred to as blowfish, pufferfish or balloonfish. In addition to the ability to inflate, blowfish have bodies covered with pointed spines. The combination makes the usually slow-moving fish a less appealing target for predators.

Most of these fish fall within the Tetraodontidae family. Possibly the most well known, the porcupine fish—pictured to the right—is the sole species with its own family, Diodontidae.

C P O G X H A W N Y R V M B Q Z K S
X A I V L O G G E R H E A D W A N L
A E B W T A I E G U E Q R L T A W E
P R I A U E F W V N I A W O O N R A
U C K Y L A A L O M U I V P B P K Z
I A T L P E W M E U A E K P L D A C
K H O U A A E R I C A P A C O R A L
O O R I S N F N A P V D K O W E N O
W R B X A V F O R I C K O R F N U W
E C M T O K I C U W O X N Y I C N N
R A I W I M S T R A X N E L S Q E F
T C R P O R P O I S E D W O H S U I
U I B E T O U P I E L A H U L E R S
P A C O P C R U S T A C E A N Y L H
E T I W D F W S U P A S N W E A K U

Can you find the words on this list in the jumble of letters above?

BLOWFISH
BALEEN
CORAL
ANEMONE
LOGGERHEAD
CRUSTACEAN
OCTOPUS
CLOWNFISH
PORPOISE
ORCA

Clownfish

This orange-and-white-striped fish is named for its waddle-like movement. Clownfish are one of only a few species of fish that can avoid the dangerous stings of the sea anemone. Staying among the anemones keeps clownfish safe from predators who can't approach without being stung by the anemone. In return, the clownfish cleans the anemone by eating the plankton that accumulate on it.

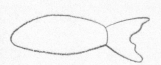  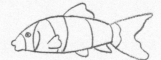 

Draw a school of clownfish among the sea anemones.

This clownfish has wandered too far from the safety of the anemones.

Help him find a way home though the battery of barracuda.

Seahorse

Unique in appearance, seahorses have an upright posture, bony body, prehensile tail, snout, and a horselike head and neck from which they get their name. They have thin skin stretched over rings of bony plates covering the length of their bodies. There are more than 40 different species of seahorse, which range from approximately 0.5 to 14 inches in length.

Seahorses' unconventional posture and small fins keep them from moving quickly or far. They are generally found resting with their tails wrapped around a stationary object like seagrass or coral.

Add more seahorses to this herd.

Unscramble the animal names on this page.
(Clue: they're all featured in this book.)

A L R A H W N

S B F O I H L W

P R E P I O O S

H A O S S H E E

N F C O I H L S W

A A R U A C R B D

O L P T I   L A H W E

R H O S S O H E E   R B A C

D M H A E M R A H E   R S K A H

D T K E R E C L H A A   E T R T L U

Can you find the
differences in
these pictures?

(there are 14 in all)

aboral surface—the top of an urchin is covered in spines that generally range from 0.4 to 1.2 inches long, but can reach up to 12 inches.

oral surface—a small mouth and surrounding fleshy area are visible on the underside of an urchin.

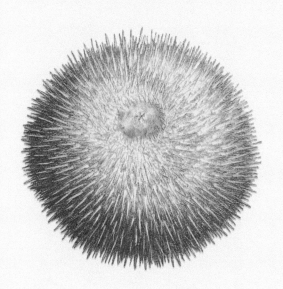

test—urchins' shells are clearly divided into five equally sized segments.

Sea Urchin

The spiny, spherical sea urchin has a shell, or test, covering most of its body. Spines, connected to rounded tubercles on the shell, cover almost all of the urchin's body. Hundreds of tiny adhesive tube feet protrude from five grooves along the animals' underside, and they use these to move, capture food, and hold onto the seafloor. The five distinctive parts radiating from the center of an urchin test show its relation to another member of the phylum Echinodermata, the sea star.

aboral surface

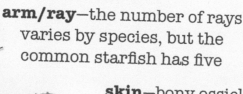

arm/ray—the number of rays varies by species, but the common starfish has five

skin—bony ossicles within the skin create a rough surface

spines—short bony spines cover the starfish's body in a pattern

eyespot—there is a simple eye located on the tip of each ray

oral surface—mouth area

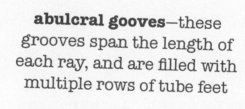

abulcral gooves—these grooves span the length of each ray, and are filled with multiple rows of tube feet

mouth—in order to compensate for its small mouth size, a starfish will push its stomach out of its mouth and digest prey externally

Starfish

One of the more recognizable creatures on the seafloor, the starfish—or sea star—can be found throughout the world's oceans at a wide variety of depths.

A relative of the sea urchin, the starfish's body components are very similar. It has the same mouth structure and abulcral grooves filled with tube feet. A starfish's diet consists mostly of clams, oysters, arthropods, gastropod mollusks, and small fish. The starfish is able to consume prey larger than its small mouth by pushing its stomach out of its body.

Known for regenerative healing abilities, some species of starfish are able to regrow entire limbs. Certain species can even grow a new body for the removed limb.

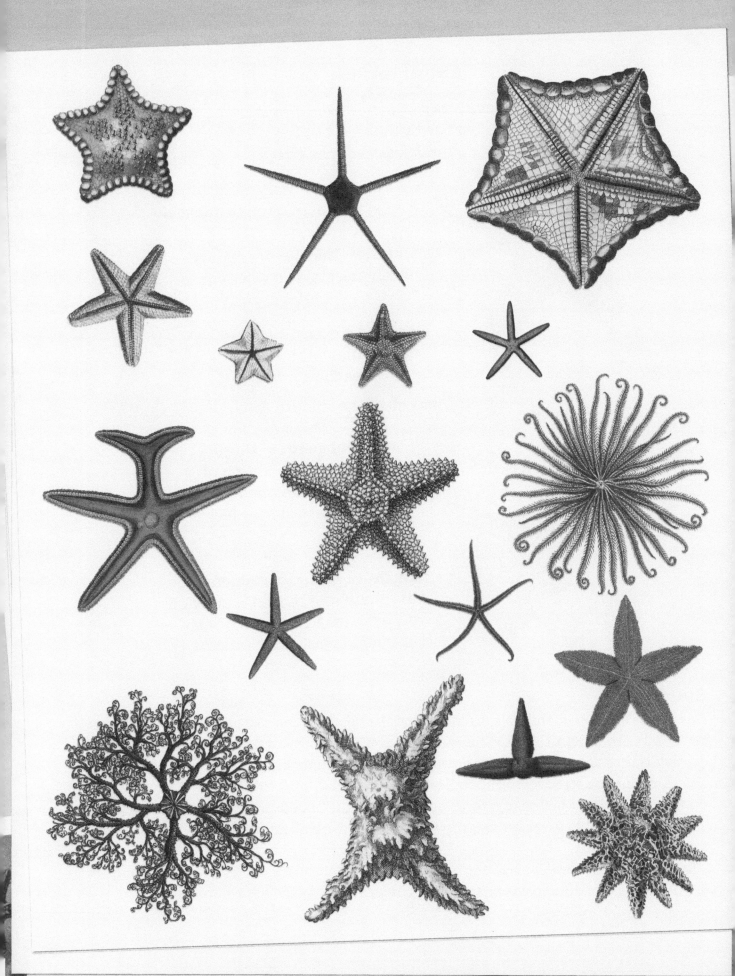

There are approximately 1,800 different species of starfish, and each has its own unique look. Draw a few of your own starfish. Chances are, they'll be similar to one of the many species out there.

Decapods

The order Decapoda includes ten-legged crustaceans, including crabs, lobsters, prawns, and shrimp. There are more than 14,000 recorded species of decapods, nearly half of which are crabs.

Blue Crab

There are numerous species identified as "blue crabs" around the world. They have flattened hind legs, which they use for paddling through open water.

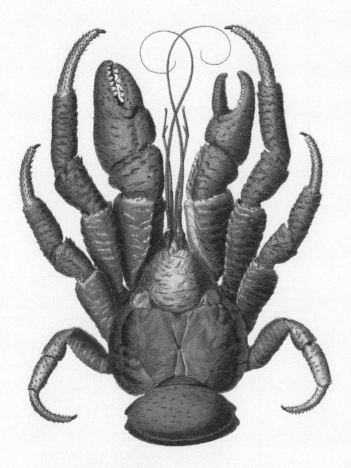

Fiddler Crab

There are approximately 100 species of the small fiddler crab (less than 2 inches wide), which is easily identified by the males' one oversized claw.

Coconut Crab

A species of land-dwelling hermit crab, the coconut crab is the largest land-living arthropod in the world, with a body length up to 16 inches long.

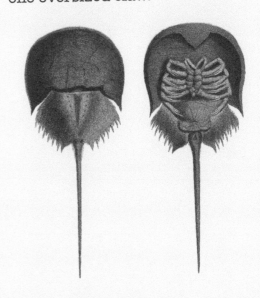

Horseshoe Crab

The alien-like horseshoe crab isn't a crab at all. It isn't even a crustacean. This living fossil is more closely related to a spider.

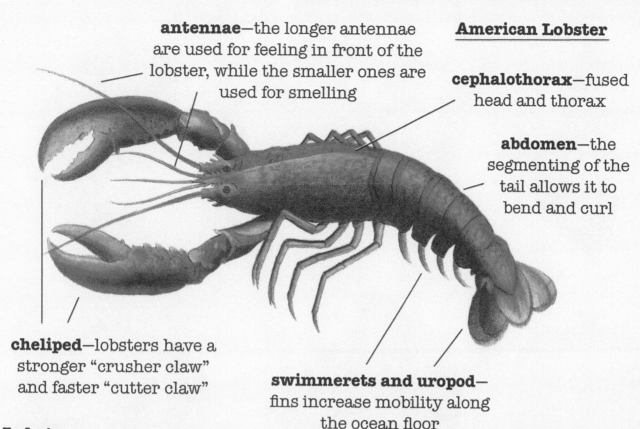

antennae—the longer antennae are used for feeling in front of the lobster, while the smaller ones are used for smelling

cephalothorax—fused head and thorax

abdomen—the segmenting of the tail allows it to bend and curl

cheliped—lobsters have a stronger "crusher claw" and faster "cutter claw"

swimmerets and uropod— fins increase mobility along the ocean floor

Lobster

Lobsters are omnivores, meaning they eat both live prey, such as fish, mollusks, and other crustaceans, as well as plant life. They generally live in crevices or burrows, preying on any food that falls into their area. After molting, they will eat their own discarded shell.

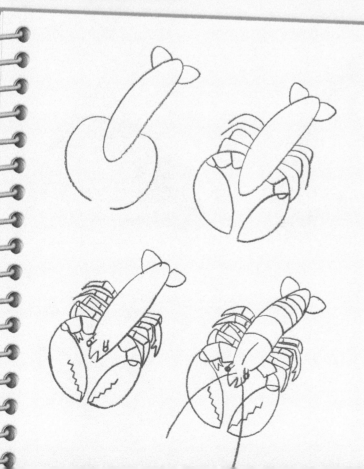

Draw a lobster.

31

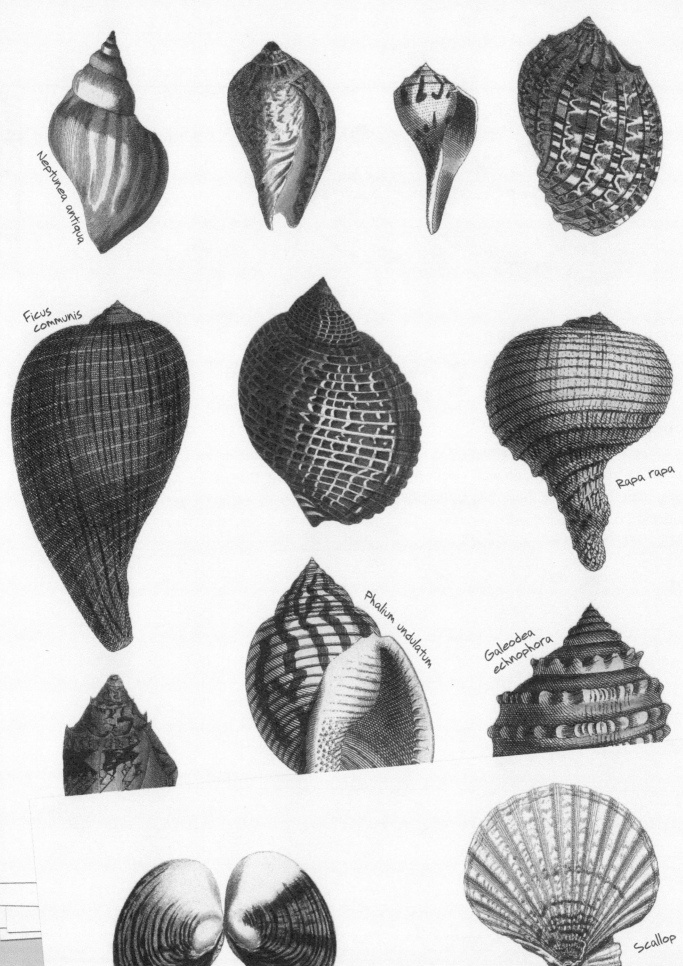

Neptunea antiqua

Ficus communis

Rapa rapa

Phalium undulatum

Galeodea echinophora

Scallop

Hermit Crabs

Hermit crabs' bodies lack a shell, leaving them
vulnerable to predators. They make up for this
by moving into discarded gastropod (snail) shells.
As the crabs grow, they need to find bigger
and bigger shells to move into.

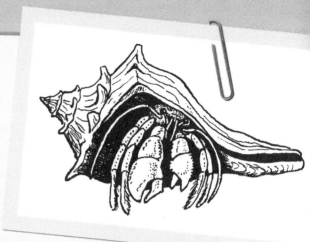

Draw a hermit crab in the
discarded shells below.

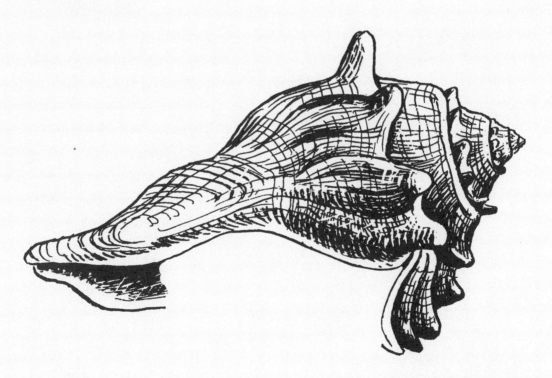

Sharks

A group of fish, sharks are identified by their cartilage skeleton, five to seven gills, and distinctive pectoral fins. Oddly, they are closely related to rays, and share many physical similarities.

Well known for their ferociousness, many sharks are the apex predators of their habitat, meaning they are at the top of the food chain, with no predators of their own.

Possibly the most well known of all sharks, the great white shark is an extremely aggressive predator. The species reaches over 20 feet long. With an enormous mouth of numerous rows of sharp, serrated teeth, it's capable of taking large bites out of prey as large as whales (there is no larger prey).

The bonnethead shark or shovelhead is a kind of hammerhead shark, easily identified by its distinctive head shape. The purpose of the head shape (called a cephalofoil) is unknown, but it's suspected to enhance the shark's smelling ability and other directional senses.

At 3 to 5 feet long, it is one of the smaller hammerheads.

Zebra sharks are one of the more docile species of shark. They are nocturnal and sit motionless on the ocean floor during the day. At night, they hunt for mollusks, crustaceans, and small fish along the ocean floor.

Whale Shark

The largest non-whale animal on earth, the whale shark reaches up to 40 feet long! Unlike most of the well-known sharks, though, it is a docile filter feeder (more like a whale), and has eating habits similar to those of the manta ray. The two animals can be found migrating together throughout the tropical oceans of the world.

Can you find the two jellyfish that don't match the others?

GRID DRAWING Draw each of these squares in its corresponding space on the next page.

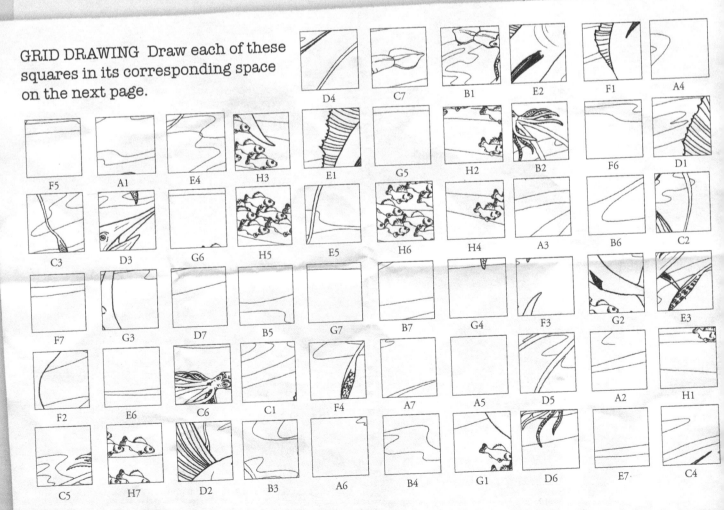

	1	2	3	4	5	6	7
A							
B							
C							
D							
E							
F							
G							
H							

Sailfish

The sailfish is one of three billfish—along with marlins and swordfish—named for their prominent sword-like bill. The sailfish has been documented at speeds of up to 68 mph, the fastest sea creature ever recorded. In addition to its bill, it also has a large, sail-like dorsal fin, which can be folded up and down, covering the length of its back. Sailfish are generally gray or brown in color, but can transform themselves into a vibrant blue almost instantly.

They feed on smaller fish and squid, which they're able to confuse and herd using their unique physical features.

Anatomy of a Sea Turtle

carapace—
top part of shell

plastron—
bottom part of shell
(not pictured)

scutes—large
horny plates that
cover the shell

Head and legs are
not retractable

Some turtles, like the loggerhead
and hawksbill, have small claws
on their fins

Sea Turtles

There are seven living species of
sea turtles: the hawksbill, flatback,
green, loggerhead, Kemp's ridley,
olive ridley, and leatherback. The
flatback sea turtle is only found
off the northern coast of Australia.
The others can be found throughout
the world, with the exception of the
Arctic and Southern oceans, which
are too cold. All of the species other
than the loggerhead are of the same
family and are physically similar, reaching 2 to 4 feet in length.

The leatherback, as well as other sea turtles, eat jellyfish, to whose sting they have developed an immunity.

Leatherback Turtle

The leatherback turtle (sometimes called the lute turtle) is the largest of all turtles and the fourth largest reptile, reaching up to ten feet long! Unlike other turtles, it doesn't have a bony shell. Instead, it has a thick, leathery skin. The most hydrodynamic of all sea turtles, the leatherback turtle is also the fastest reptile on earth, reaching up to 22mph.

Sea turtles will travel great distances in their lifetime, spanning oceans.

The migratory route here is common among Atlantic loggerheads.

From Egg to Ocean

The most treacherous part of a sea turtle's life is its initial trip to the sea after hatching.

Turtles instinctively hatch at night and race to the sea before sunrise; after the sun comes up, they only have a 1% chance of survival. Hatchlings will take days to dig to the surface from their buried eggs, sprint to the sea, and then quickly ride the undertow to deep water, away from predators. Only 1 in 100 reaches adulthood.

These hatchlings have emerged during the day and the beach is full of hungry predators.

Help them find their way to the safety of the ocean.

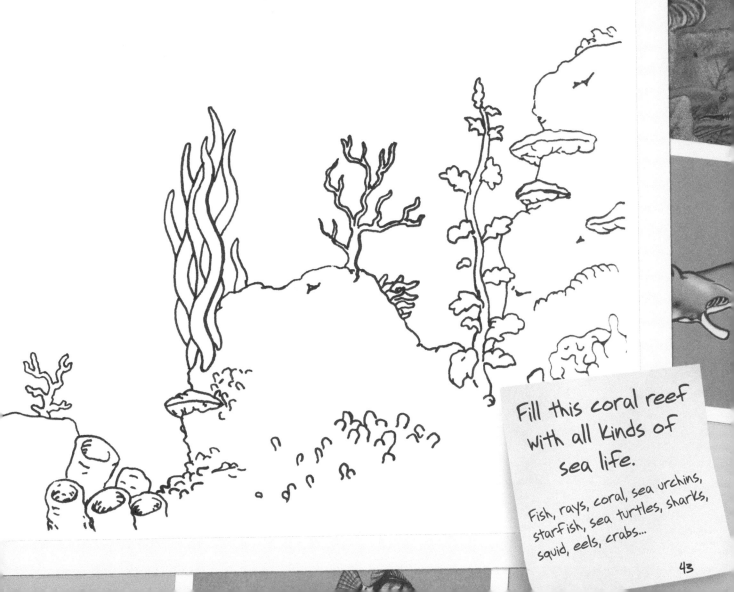

Fill this coral reef
with all kinds of
sea life.

Fish, rays, coral, sea urchins,
starfish, sea turtles, sharks,
squid, eels, crabs...

SOLUTIONS

Moray Eel - 1, **Urchin - 6**, **Moorish Idol - 5**, **Clownfish - 11**, Seahorse - 3, **Scallop - 3**, Anemone - 6, **Starfish - 6**, Butterflyfish - 5

Pages 12-13

```
C P O G X H A W N Y R V M B Q Z K S
X A I V L O G G E R H E A D W A N L
A E B W T A I E G U E Q R L T A W E
P R I A U E F W V N I A W O O N R A
U C K Y L A A L O M U I V P B P K Z
I A T L P E W M E U A E K P L D A C
K H O U A A E R I C A P A C O R A L
O O R I S N F N A P V D K O W E N O
W R B X A V F O R I C K O R F N U W
E C M T O K I C U W O X N Y I C N N
R A I W I M S T R A X N E L S Q E F
T C R P O R P O I S E D W O H S U I
U I B E T O U P I E L A H U L E R S
P A C O P C R U S T A C E A N Y L H
E T I W D F W S U P A S N W E K U L
```

Page 19

44

Page 21

N A R W H A L
A L R A H W N

B L O W F I S H
S B F O I H L W

P O R P O I S E
P R E P I O O S

N A R W H A L
H A O S S H E E

C L O W N F I S H
N F C O I H L S W

B A R R A C U D A
A A R U A C R B D

P I L O T W H A L E
O L P T I L A H W E

H O R S E S H O E C R A B
R H O S S O H E E R B A C

H A M M E R H E A D S H A R K
D M H A E M R A H E R S K A H

L E A T H E R B A C K T U R T L E
D T K E R E C L H A A E T R T L U

Page 23

Pages 24-25

Page 36

Pages 36-37

Page 41

Clownfish

Seahorse

Scallop

Anemones

Butterflyfish